Chasing Fire

anestassia yu

BookLeaf Publishing

India | USA | UK

Made with ❤ on the BookLeaf Publishing Platform
www.bookleafpub.in
www.bookleafpub.com

Dedication

healing from 109

Preface

Acknowledgements

1.

like a moth to a flame
i chase you
knowing all too well
i will be burned

2.

he was the heat in my winter
i was the cold in his summer
we both knew this was seasonal
we were on borrowed time

3.

the inner workings of your mind
i thought was pure poetry.
now i only hear
incoherent, ordinary,
nothingness.
just empty words that fill the air.

4.

how do you protect a heart that is not your own but
everyone else's?
a heart that constantly gives and rarely takes
a heart that is there for everyone
but never there for itself

5.

i crave you

like sunflowers turn to the sun
like bumblebees search for honey

like lips yearning to be kissed
like hands wanting to be held

like the light lives for the day
like the dark sleeps for the night

like the pillow to my head
like the covers to my bed

like an orchestra plays its symphony
like a conductor leads the harmony

i crav**ed** you

6.

6

every time i think of you
a fire ignites inside of me

i get angry
i get depressed

and even after all of that,
i just want to fall into your arms

and get burned
over and over again

until enough tears extinguish the flames
and all is left is a burnt memory of you

7.

when i got to know your soul
there was a combustion in my heart
that rearranged all my parts
and now the fire has been tamed
blown out, a ceasefire
i am left with nothing but
burnt and broken pieces

8.

i was your ashtray
collecting the mere butts of what was left
from the love you gave everyone else
but me

9.

did you forget?
or just not care?

no, you wanted to hurt me.

-my birthday

10.

the pursuit was a tug of war
elusive, futile
reckless but exciting
passionate but destructive

how do you catch a flame
without it burning out,
when it feels impossible to grasp?

11.

you were the lighter
that ignited my insecurities
bringing to flames my self-identity
and leaving a shell of a person.

12.

you were the shot of espresso
i thought i needed in the morning
your arms were the fortresses
i thought i was searching for

instead all i found were
burnt ashes and hollow walls

13.

i thought you were my home
warm, calm, safe,
my gentle reminder to breathe

but you sucked up all the air in the room
suffocating every thought, every piece of me.

-a firecracker disguised as a fireplace

14.

you exhausted the warmth from my flames
to feed your fractured ego

you shattered my identity
as a desperate attempt
to find an internal sense of self

and in the end, you harmed the person who loved you,
you burned bridges with the person who would have
given you the world.

-narcissist

15.

you described it as
a "once in a lifetime" kind of love
but maybe you were wrong,
maybe just not in this lifetime

16.

your words were putrid potpourri
disguising your whispers of sweet nothings
promised through tainted lips

17.

if walls could talk
they would say to run
after watching you erode
every part of me.

people could call you a sculptor
after seeing you chip away the effervescence,
shining from the pieces of me,
dulling and refining the vision
you wanted, you created
in your head.

18.

18

being in love with you
felt like my body was on drugs
constantly intoxicated, addicting
looking for the next high.

now, my body and soul are in withdrawal,
rewiring itself to unlearn you
your touch, your presence,
the familiarity of you

19.

being loved by you felt like a wildfire
scorching my world,
stripping it of all its beauty
the way whiskey leaves
a burning rage in your throat

20.

chasing fire is like living in ignorance
it is blissful, cozy, warm
until it is disrupted by reality
and burns your life to the ground

21.

in due time,
i will stop chasing
this fire that is the idea of
loving you and being loved by you
and be reborn
from the ashes of the memory of you,
burning brighter than ever.